Common Core Connections
Language Arts

Grade K

Carson-Dellosa Publishing, LLC
Greensboro, North Carolina

Credits
Content Editor: Jeanette M. Ritch, M.S. Ed.
Copy Editor: Carrie D'Ascoli

 Visit *carsondellosa.com* for correlations to Common Core, state, national, and Canadian provincial standards.

Carson-Dellosa Publishing, LLC
PO Box 35665
Greensboro, NC 27425 USA
carsondellosa.com

Table of Contents

Introduction

What are the Common Core State Standards for English Language Arts?

The standards are a shared set of expectations for each grade level in the areas of reading, writing, speaking, listening, and language. They define what students should understand and be able to do. The standards are designed to be more rigorous and allow for students to justify their thinking. They reflect the knowledge that is necessary for success in college and beyond.

As described in the Common Core State Standards, students who master the standards in reading, writing, speaking, listening, and language as they advance through the grades will exhibit the following capabilities:

1. They demonstrate independence.
2. They build strong content knowledge.
3. They respond to the varying demands of audience, task, purpose, and discipline.
4. They comprehend as well as critique.
5. They value evidence.
6. They use technology and digital media strategically and capably.
7. They come to understand other perspectives and cultures.*

How to Use This Book

This book is a collection of practice pages aligned to the Common Core State Standards for English Language Arts and appropriate for kindergarten. Included is a skill matrix so that you can see exactly which standards are addressed on the practice pages. Also included are a skill assessment and a skill assessment analysis. Use the assessment at the beginning of the year or at any time of year you wish to assess your students' mastery of certain standards. The analysis connects each test item to a practice page or set of practice pages so that you can review skills with students who struggle in certain areas.

* © Copyright 2010. National Governors Association Center for Best Practices and Council of Chief State School Officers. All rights reserved.

Common Core State Standards*
Alignment Matrix

Pages	12	13	14	15	16	17	18	19	20	21	22	23	24	25	26	27	28	29	30	31	32	33	34	35	36	37	38	39	40	41	42	43	44	45	46	47	48	49	50	51
K.RL.1	●	●																																						
K.RL.2			●																																					
K.RL.3				●																																				
K.RL.4					●																																			
K.RL.5						●	●																																	
K.RL.6								●																																
K.RL.7									●																															
K.RL.9											●																													
K.RL.10												●	●																											
K.RI.1														●																										
K.RI.2													●																											
K.RI.3															●	●																								
K.RI.4																	●																							
K.RI.5																		●																						
K.RI.6																			●																					
K.RI.7																				●																				
K.RI.8																					●																			
K.RI.9																						●																		
K.RI.10																							●																	
K.RF.1																								●																
K.RF.1a																								●																
K.RF.1b																									●	●	●													
K.RF.1c																												●	●	●										
K.RF.1d																															●	●								
K.RF.2																																		●						
K.RF.2a																																			●	●	●			
K.RF.2b																																	●							
K.RF.2c																																						●		
K.RF.2d																																		●					●	●
K.RF.2e																																								
K.RF.3																																								
K.RF.3a																																								
K.RF.3b																																								
K.RF.3c																																								
K.RF.3d																																								
K.RF.4																																								
K.W.1																																								
K.W.2																																								
K.W.3																																								
K.W.5																																								
K.W.6																																								
K.W.7																																								
K.W.8																																								
K.L.1																																								
K.L.1a																															●	●								
K.L.1b																																								
K.L.1c																																								
K.L.1d																																								
K.L.1e																																								
K.L.1f																																								
K.L.2																																								
K.L.2a																																								
K.L.2b																																								
K.L.2c																																								
K.L.2d																																	●							
K.L.4																																								
K.L.4a																																								
K.L.4b																																								
K.L.5																																								
K.L.5a																																								
K.L.5b																																								
K.L.5c																																								
K.L.5d																																								
K.L.6																																								

Common Core State Standards*
Alignment Matrix

Pages	52	53	54	55	56	57	58	59	60	61	62	63	64	65	66	67	68	69	70	71	72	73	74	75	76	77	78	79	80	81	82	83	84	85	86	87	88	89	90
K.RL.1																																							
K.RL.2																																							
K.RL.3																																							
K.RL.4																																							
K.RL.5																																							
K.RL.6																																							
K.RL.7																																							
K.RL.9																																							
K.RL.10																																							
K.RI.1																																							
K.RI.2																																							
K.RI.3																																							
K.RI.4																																							
K.RI.5																																							
K.RI.6																																							
K.RI.7																																							
K.RI.8																																							
K.RI.9																																							
K.RI.10																																							
K.RF.1																																							
K.RF.1a																																							
K.RF.1b																																							
K.RF.1c																																							
K.RF.1d																																							
K.RF.2																																							
K.RF.2a		•																																					
K.RF.2b																																							
K.RF.2c			•																																				
K.RF.2d	•																																						
K.RF.2e		•	•																																				
K.RF.3				•	•																																		
K.RF.3a						•																																	
K.RF.3b							•																																
K.RF.3c								•	•																														
K.RF.3d										•																													
K.RF.4											•																												
K.W.1												•	•																										
K.W.2													•																										
K.W.3															•	•																							
K.W.5																	•	•																					
K.W.6																			•	•	•																		
K.W.7																						•	•																
K.W.8																								•															
K.L.1												•	•	•																									
K.L.1a																																							
K.L.1b																									•														
K.L.1c																										•													
K.L.1d																						•					•												
K.L.1e																												•											
K.L.1f																													•										
K.L.2																						•	•																
K.L.2a																														•									
K.L.2b																														•									
K.L.2c		•	•																																				
K.L.2d																																							
K.L.4																																	•						
K.L.4a																																		•					
K.L.4b																																			•				
K.L.5																																			•				
K.L.5a																																				•			
K.L.5b																																					•		
K.L.5c																																						•	
K.L.5d																																						•	•
K.L.6																																							•

6

© Carson-Dellosa • CD-104607

Name_____

Will and Mia are best friends. They like many of the same things. They like to ride bikes. They walk the dog together. They play outside on the **swing set**. A swing set is a small playground.

Will and Mia like different things too. Will likes to climb trees. Mia likes to play soccer. Will likes to use chalk. Mia likes to jump rope. They are still best friends!

1. What do Will and Mia both like to do?

_____

2. What does Mia like to do?

_____

3. What is a **swing set**?

_____

4. Who likes to climb trees?

_____

Tigers are the largest wildcats in the world! They have red and orange fur. They have black stripes. They like to hunt for food. They hunt at night. They use their big claws. They can eat a lot of meat! Tigers are great swimmers. They like to cool off in the water.

Tigers are beautiful but **endangered**. This means they are hunted too much. Now, tigers are being helped. People help tigers and their **cubs**. Cubs are baby tigers. Save the tigers!

5. What does **endangered** mean?

_____

6. What are **cubs**?

_____

7. How does the author feel about tigers?

_____

8. Write the alphabet.

Uppercase Letters

Lowercase Letters

Name_____

9. Write three words that rhyme with **mat**.

10. How many syllables are in each word?

Words	Number of Syllables
teacher	
number	
name	

11. Write each word in the correct column.

bike bin dime dish fun game home pane run tin

Short Vowel Words	Long Vowel Words

12. Write a sentence about your favorite book.

_____

_____

13. Complete the chart.

Noun – person, place, thing, or idea	**Verb** – action word
van	run

14. Make each noun plural.

rake _____   bike _____

car _____   toy _____

15. This sentence has three mistakes.

my cousin and i will see my grandma

Write the sentence correctly.

_____

16. Name three places in school that are colorful.

After you review your student's skill assessment, match those problems answered incorrectly to the Common Core State Standards below. Pay special attention to the pages that fall into these problem sections, and ensure that your student receives supervision in these areas. In this way, your student will strengthen these skills.

Answer Key:
1. They like to ride bikes, play on the swing set, and walk the dog. 2. She likes to play soccer and jumps rope. 3. small playground; 4. Will; 5. hunted too much; 6. baby tigers; 7. The author wants to save the tigers. 8. Check students' letters. 9. Answers will vary but may include at, bat, cat, fat, hat, Nat, pat, or that. 10. 2, 2, 1; 11. short vowel words: bin, fish, fun, run, tin; long vowel words: bike, dime, game, home, pane; 12. Answers will vary but should include a subject and verb. 13. Answers will vary. 14. rakes, bikes, cars, toys; 15. My cousin and I will see my grandma. 16. Answers will vary.

Common Core State Standards*		Test Items	Practice Pages
Reading Standards for Literature			
Key Ideas and Details	K.RL.1–K.RL.3	1, 2, 4	12–15
Craft and Structure	K.RL.4	3	16
Reading Standards for Informational Text			
Key Ideas and Details	K.RI.1–K.RI.2	5–7	24, 25
Craft and Structure	K.RI.4	5, 6	28
Integration of Knowledge and Ideas	K.RI.8	7	32
Reading Standards: Foundational Skills			
Print Concepts	K.RF.1	8	35–43
Phonological Awareness	K.RF.2	9, 10	44–54
Phonics and Word Recognition	K.RF.3	11	55–61
Writing Standards			
Text Types and Purposes	K.W.1	12	63, 64
Language Standards			
Conventions of Standard English	K.L.1–K.L.2	13–15	42–44, 53, 54, 63–65, 73–81
Vocabulary Acquisition and Use	K.L.5	16	88

* © Copyright 2010. National Governors Association Center for Best Practices and Council of Chief State School Officers. All rights reserved.

Read the story.

   Mom told Ryan it was time to go. Ryan put on his shoes. He put on his jacket. Then, he put on his coat. Ryan got into the car. Mom and Ryan went to the store.

   Ryan asked Mom where they were going. Mom said it was a surprise. She drove into the lot. She found a good spot for the car. She parked the car. Ryan took off his seat belt. He opened the door. It was the grocery store!

   Ryan held Mom's hand. He was happy! He wanted to buy his favorite kind of fruit. Ryan loves oranges!

Answer the questions.

1. Who was in the car? _____

2. What does Ryan love? _____

3. Where did Mom take Ryan? _____

4. When did Ryan open the door? _____

5. How does Ryan feel? _____

☐   I can read a story.
☐   I can answer questions.

Use the story details to answer the questions.

1. Bill has a big, red car.
   It can go fast.
   Bill likes to go fast in his car.

   What color is Bill's car? _____

2. Dogs are fun pets.
   They run and play with you.
   They chase the balls and sticks you throw.

   What do dogs chase? _____

3. It is good to keep clean.
   You should wash your hands often.
   You should brush your teeth every day.
   You should take baths too.

   What should you brush every day? _____

☐ **I can read a story and answer detailed questions.**

Read the story. Answer the questions.

The Boy Who Cried Wolf

There was a boy on the hill. His village was quiet and peaceful. He was in charge of the sheep. He watched them and watched them. He became bored. He yelled, "Help! A wolf!"

The people in the village ran to help the boy. When they got there, they did not see a wolf. The sheep were eating grass. The boy smiled. The villagers told the boy not to cry wolf. They left.

The villagers got to the bottom of the hill. The boy yelled again. "Help! A wolf!" The villagers ran back. They did not see a wolf. The boy laughed. The villagers told the boy not to cry wolf. They were angry now.

The villagers got to the bottom of the hill. The boy saw a wolf. This time, he was scared. The wolf was near the sheep. He cried, "Help! A wolf!" The villagers did not go back.

The boy ran to the villagers. He said the sheep ran away. The sheep were scared of the wolf. The villagers said they did not believe the boy. He told them the wolf really came. He was sorry for pretending there was a wolf before. The villagers would have helped him this time.

1. What did the boy do at the beginning of the story?

_____

2. What did the boy do at the end of the story?

_____

3. Why did the villagers not help the boy?

_____

❑   I can read a story.
❑   I can retell a story.
❑   I can retell details of a story.

14

Read the story on page 14. Fill in the boxes.

1. Draw pictures of the **characters**, or people, in the story.	
2. Draw a picture of the **setting**. The setting is where the story takes place.	
3. Draw a picture of an **event** in the story. An event is something that happens in the story.	

❑   **I can name the characters.**
❑   **I can draw the setting.**
❑   **I can understand events in a story.**

Read the story. Look at the bold words. Answer the questions.

The sun was out. Sally wanted to go outside. She needed to water her plants. She put on her garden gloves. She put on her boots. She went outside. She got water.

Sally went to the flower bed. She watered the **marigolds**. They smelled strong. She pushed the **soil** around the flowers. Her gloves got dirty!

Sally went to the herb garden. She watered the **basil** plants. They smelled fresh! Sally picked a few leaves.

Sally brought the leaves inside. She showed her big sister. She will make dinner. She will add basil to the sauce. It will taste great!

1. What is a marigold? _____

2. What is soil? _____

3. What is basil? _____

☐ I can understand words in a story.
☐ I can look at the text to define words I do not know.

Read the poem.

The cars drive by,
I sit and look,
The birds come and sing,
I read a book.

The mailman arrives,
I get a letter,
The cool wind blows,
I put on my sweater.

The neighbor is home,
I wave good day,
The hot sun shines,
I think I will play.

My porch is where I sit,
I like to rest,
My porch is where I look,
I like it here best.

What did you see when you read the poem? Draw a picture.

❏ I can read poetry.
❏ I can read a poem with rhyme.
❏ I can draw a picture about a poem.

A **story** tells a tale. A story has characters. A story has a setting. Events take place. A **poem** can also tell a story. A poem can have a setting. Events can take place. A poem often has rhyming words. A poem may not have complete sentences. A story and a poem are alike and different.

Answer each question.

1. How are a story and a poem alike?

_____

_____

2. How are a story and a poem different?

_____

_____

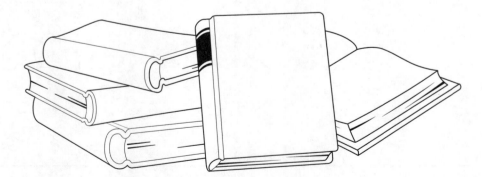

❑   I can understand how a story and a poem are alike.
❑   I can understand how a story and a poem are different.
❑   I can read different texts.

K.RL.6

The Great Book Look

Find three books in your classroom or library.
Look at the front cover of each book.
Complete the chart.

1. What is the name of the book? Write the book's **title**.	2. Who wrote the book? Write the name of the **author**.	3. Who drew the pictures? Write the name of the **illustrator**.
_____ _____	_____ _____	_____ _____
_____ _____	_____ _____	_____ _____
_____ _____	_____ _____	_____ _____

❑ **I can find a title of a book.**
❑ **I can find an author of the book.**
❑ **I can find an illustrator of the book.**

Read the story. Answer the questions.

The Twins

Kim and Kris are twins. They like to do a lot of the same things. They both like to jump rope. They both like to swim. They both ride bikes.

But, even twins like to do some things differently. The girls dress differently. Kris likes to wear shorts. Kim wears skirts. Kris likes bows in her hair. Kim likes her hair down. Kris likes to wear a belt. Kim wears sandals.

Both girls think it is fun to have a twin.

1. What do both girls like to do?

_____

The girls also like different things. Make a list for each girl.

2. Kris likes to . . .	3. Kim likes to . . .

☐ **I can compare and contrast characters in a story.**

Read the story. Compare and contrast the characters. How are they alike? How are they different?

The Race

The hare wanted to run in a race. The hare told a turtle how fast he was. "Do you want to race?" the hare asked. The turtle nodded his head.

The two went to a path in the woods. It was time to race! The hare and the turtle began. The hare ran fast. The turtle walked slowly. The hare was ahead of the turtle. The hare got tired. He sat and rested. Soon, he fell asleep!

The turtle kept walking. He walked slowly, but he was steady. He walked by the hare. He saw the hare was asleep. The turtle walked on.

The hare woke up. He stood up and ran. He knew he would win the race. He got to the finish line. He saw the turtle. The turtle was waiting for him! The turtle won.

Slow and steady wins the race.

1. How do you think the hare looked at the finish line? Draw a picture.	2. How do you think the turtle looked at the finish line? Draw a picture.

3. **Compare** the hare and the turtle. How are they **alike**?

_____

4. **Contrast** the hare and the turtle. How are they **different**?

_____

❑   **I can compare and contrast characters in a story.**

Read the play with two partners. There are three characters in this play. Each person in your group will choose a character. Read the lines for your character.

The Big Truck

Dad: It is time to go, Lin.

Lin: Where are we going?

Dad: We are going to look at trucks.

Jake: I want to go too!

Dad: You can come too, Jake.

Lin: This will be fun!

Jake: Why do we need to look at trucks?

Lin: I wanted to ask that too.

Jake: Are we going to buy a truck?

Dad: Yes!

Draw the truck that Lin, Jake, and Dad took home.

❑   I can actively read.
❑   I can read in a group.
❑   I can read with purpose.

Read the play with two partners. There are three characters in this play. Each person in your group will choose a character. Read the lines for your character.

Inside the Barn

Farmer: Welcome to the farm!

Allie: We are glad we came.

Yasmin: You have so many animals here.

Farmer: Yes. We have more than 20 kinds of animals.

Allie: What is that red house over there?

Farmer: It is a barn.

Yasmin: What is in the barn?

Allie: It looks scary.

Farmer: It is a nice place for the cows to rest. Let's go!

Yasmin: That is a great idea!

Draw the barn.

❏ I can actively read.
❏ I can read in a group.
❏ I can read with purpose.

Read the passage.

Black and White Stripes

What animal has black and white stripes? A skunk is black. It has a white stripe. But, a zebra has many black stripes and white stripes! Each zebra has its own stripes. No two zebras are alike.

Zebras like to be with each other. They live in groups. The groups are called **herds**. They love to eat grass. Zebras have to watch for lions and hyenas. Lions and hyenas hunt zebras. Zebras stay next to each other. Zebras take care of each other.

1. Go back to the passage. Underline a sentence with one new fact you learned.

2. Write the sentence.

_____

_____

3. Share your fact with a friend.

❏ **I can read text with facts.**
❏ **I can retell details.**

Read the passage. Answer the questions.

The School Playground

Many schools have playgrounds. Playgrounds are for kids to play on. Some kids use them at recess time. Other kids play on them after school or on the weekends. Playgrounds have many parts. Many have slides. The slides can be short or long. There may be monkey bars and ladders. A playground can have a sandbox. School playgrounds are fun!

1. What is this passage about? _____

2. Name four parts of the playground.

3. What part would you like to add? _____

_____

❑ **I can read text with facts.**
❑ **I can find key details.**
❑ **I can answer questions about text with facts.**

Words have a **connection**. One idea or sentence can be linked to another. **Events** in a story have a connection. They are connected to a **cause**. A cause tells what made an event happen in the story.

What made these events happen? Write the letter of the cause next to the correct event.

Events

_____ 1. Justin put on his hat and mittens.

_____ 2. Sally put water in the tub.

_____ 3. Ken gave his dog a toy.

_____ 4. The rabbit ate the carrot.

Causes

A. It was snowing.

B. It was hungry.

C. She wanted a bath.

D. The dog liked to play.

❑ I can make a connection.
❑ I can understand the cause of an event.

A story is always about something. The title helps tell you what the story is about. Look at the pictures. Write a title for each set of pictures.

Title ___ ___ ___			
Title ___ ___ ___			
Title ___ ___ ___			
Title ___ ___ ___			

❑ **I can make a title for a story.**
❑ **I can connect words to pictures.**

Read the passage. Look at the bold words. Complete the chart.

Snakes

Not all reptiles are as big as dinosaurs! A snake is a **reptile**. A reptile is a cold-blooded animal. It has **scales**. Scales are square. They are hard. They cover a snake's body. Snakes can grow long. They live all over the world. They even live in the **rain forests**. The rain forests are warm, wet places. Snakes like to be outside.

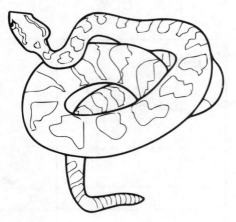

New Words	What Do They Mean?
1. reptile	
2. scales	
3. rain forest	

❑ **I can find the meaning of new words in a text.**

A book has a front cover and a back cover. The covers protect the book's pages. The front cover has important information on it. It tells the title. It may have pictures.

When you open a book, there is a title page. It is the first page of a book. It tells the title of the book. It tells who wrote the book (the author). It tells who drew the pictures (the illustrator).

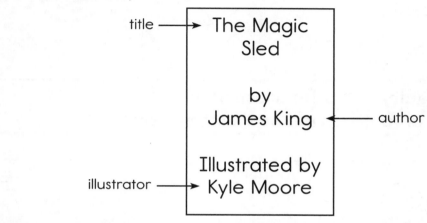

Find a book. Look at the title page. Write the title. Write the name of the author. Write the name of the illustrator.

title

by

Illustrated by

☐ **I can find the front and back cover of a book.**
☐ **I can find the title page.**

An **author** writes a book. Authors write sentences. They write about topics. An **illustrator** draws pictures. Illustrators make the art for books. They use many art tools.

Follow the directions.

1. Cut out the squares.
2. Get a pencil ready!
3. Find four books.
4. Complete the chart.

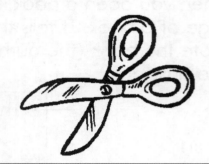

❑ I can find the author and the illustrator.
❑ I can tell what an author and an illustrator do.

Title	Title
_____	_____
Author	Author
_____	_____
Illustrator	Illustrator
_____	_____

Title	Title
_____	_____
Author	Author
_____	_____
Illustrator	Illustrator
_____	_____

What Am I?

I have a big body.
I can have brown fur.
I live in the woods.
What am I?

1._____

I live in the water.
I like to swim.
I have gills.
What am I?

2._____

I have a small body.
I have long ears.
I like to hop.
What am I?

3._____

I have many arms called tentacles.
I live in the ocean.
I have ink.
What am I?

4._____

☐ **I can understand the relationship between text and pictures.**

Are Bats Scary?

Bats come out at night. They fly in the air when it is dark. Many people think bats are scary. Are bats really scary? They are not. They are useful! <u>Bats keep bugs away from us.</u> One bat can catch hundreds of bugs in one hour. Bats help us. <u>Bats are also very interesting.</u> They cannot see well. They use their ears to help them fly in the dark. Bats are not bad after all!

The author writes reasons why bats are not scary. The reasons are underlined. Write the reasons.

1. _____

   _____

   _____

2. _____

   _____

   _____

❑ I can find the author's reasons for supporting a point.
❑ I can write an author's reasons.

Read each story about safety. Fill in the boxes.

Boys and girls ride bikes. They have to wear helmets. The ground can have a hole. Rocks can be on the road. Boys and girls have to stay safe. They do not want to hurt their heads!

Gardening gloves keep hands safe. Some flowers have sharp thorns. Gloves keep hands clean. Dirt can get under fingernails. Gloves are handy!

1. Draw yourself in a helmet.	2. Draw yourself with gloves on.

3. How are both stories the same?

_____

4. How are they different?

_____

□   I can read two texts about the same topic.
□   I can tell how two texts about the same topic are the same and different.

Find three partners. Write your names. Take turns reading each sentence in the passage.

Reader 1: _____   Reader 2: _____

Reader 3: _____   Reader 4: _____

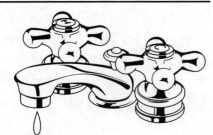

People waste water sometimes. We use water in the bathroom. Some people leave the water on. Water can drip from a broken faucet. A bath uses a lot of water. A shower does not use as much water. We do not want water to run out. We can save water when we brush our teeth. We can fix the faucet. We can take showers. It is good to save water.

Talk with your partners about these questions.

Who uses water?

What is the text about?

Where do people use water?

When do people use water?

Why should we not waste water?

How do we save water?

❑ **I can read in a group.**
❑ **I understand what I read in a group.**

> The words in a sentence are in order. They tell a thought. It is a complete sentence.
>
> Example: I like to play ball.
>
> Words that are not in order do not form a complete sentence.
>
> Example: play ball I to like

Read each groups of words. Circle the group that is a complete sentence.

1. For a ride she.

   My sister is over there.

   Ice cream.

Write the words in order. Make complete sentences.

2. seen you Have my backpack?

   _____

3. go park to the We.

   _____

❑ **I understand the basic features of print.**
❑ **I can follow words from left to right.**
❑ **I can understand complete sentences.**

Trace and read each word aloud. Write the word. Color the picture.

red

blue

yellow

green

purple

❑ I know that spoken words can be written.
❑ I know that letters make sounds.
❑ I can write words.

Trace and read each word aloud. Write the word. Color the picture.

car

train

bus

truck

boat

plane

☐ I know that spoken words can be written.
☐ I know that letters make sounds.
☐ I can write words.

Trace and read each word aloud. Write the word. Color the picture.

cat

_____

dog

_____

bird

_____

fish

_____

rabbit

_____

frog

_____

- ☐ I know that spoken words can be written.
- ☐ I know that letters make sounds.
- ☐ I can write words.

Look at each sentence. There is a space between each word. Circle the sentence that describes each picture.

I see three apples.

I see five apples.

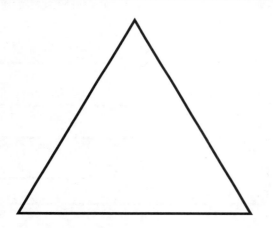

It is a rectangle.

It is a triangle.

The paint is red.

The paint is blue.

❑ **I know that words are separated by spaces.**
❑ **I can see spaces between the words in a sentence.**

Trace each sentence. Do you see the space after each word? Draw a picture of the sentence.

The car is blue.

The bird can fly.

- ❑ I can write sentences.
- ❑ I can see the spaces between words in a sentence.

Trace each sentence. Do you see the space after each word? Draw a picture of the sentence.

I like ice cream!

Write your own sentence. Make a space after each word. Draw a picture that matches the sentence.

☐ I can write a sentence.
☐ I can make a space after each word in my sentence.

K.RF.1d, K.L.1a

Write the lowercase letter next to each uppercase letter. A hint is at the bottom of the page.

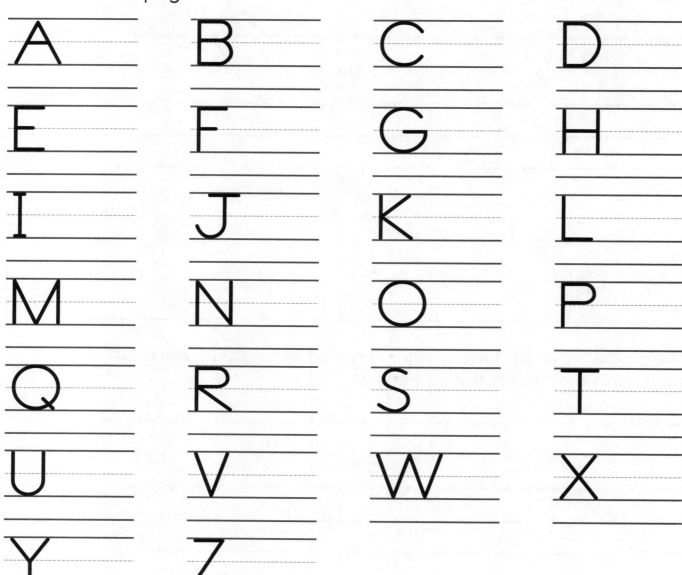

A

B

C

D

E

F

G

H

I

J

K

L

M

N

O

P

Q

R

S

T

U

V

W

X

Y

Z

Aa Bb Cc Dd Ee Ff Gg Hh Ii Jj Kk Ll Mm Nn
Oo Pp Qq Rr Ss Tt Uu Vv Ww Xx Yy Zz

☐ I can recognize all uppercase and lowercase letters of the alphabet.
☐ I can name all uppercase and lowercase letters of the alphabet.
☐ I can write all lowercase letters of the alphabet.

Write the uppercase letter next to each lowercase letter. A hint is at the bottom of the page.

a   b   c   d

e   f   g   h

i   j   k   l

m   n   o   p

q   r   s   t

u   v   w   x

y   z

Aa Bb Cc Dd Ee Ff Gg Hh Ii Jj Kk Ll Mm Nn
Oo Pp Qq Rr Ss Tt Uu Vv Ww Xx Yy Zz

❑ I an recognize all uppercase and lowercase letters of the alphabet.
❑ I can name all uppercase and lowercase letters of the alphabet.
❑ I can write all uppercase letters of the alphabet.

All words have parts. Each part is a syllable. The number of syllables in a word is the same as the number of vowel sounds in the word.

Examples: dog = one vowel sound = one syllable
happy = two vowel sounds = two syllables

Count the syllables and vowel sounds in each word.

Words	Syllables	Vowel Sounds
1. brother	2	2
2. three		
3. red		
4. sister		
5. elephant		

Words	Syllables	Vowel Sounds
6. pretty		
7. under		
8. favorite		
9. nine		
10. truck		

Look at the words above. Sort them into the correct box.

1 Syllable	2 Syllables	3 Syllables

☐ **I can count syllables.**
☐ **I can segment syllables.**

Draw lines to connect the pictures whose names rhyme. Color the pictures.

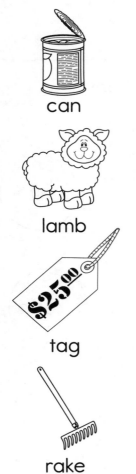

can

lamb

tag

rake

flag

fan

cake

jar

How many syllables are in each word? Write the number.

1. pancake _____   2. backpack _____   3. win _____

4. cake _____   5. pack _____   6. window _____

☐ I count syllables.
☐ I can rhyme words.
☐ I can understand sounds in words.

Name_____

Words that sound alike are called rhyming words. The beginning sounds are different.

Examples: c<u>at</u>, h<u>at</u>   s<u>it</u>, h<u>it</u>

Read the word in each bubble. Follow the directions.
1. Color the bubbles red that rhyme with *cat*.
2. Color the bubbles yellow that rhyme with *hop*.
3. Color the bubbles green that rhyme with *bed*.
4. Color the bubbles blue that rhyme with *bug*.
5. Color the boy and the dog in the bathtub.

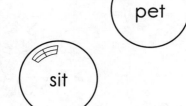

☐ I can rhyme.
☐ I can rhyme short vowel words.

46

Name_____

1. Find two pictures whose names rhyme with *snake*. Color them green.
2. Draw a blue triangle around each picture that rhymes with *stone*.
3. Cross out the pictures in the top row whose names rhyme with *lie*.
4. Find two pictures whose names rhyme with *wire*. Color them red.
5. Draw a brown circle around each picture whose name rhymes with *plate*.

☐ **I can name words that rhyme.**
☐ **I can rhyme words with long vowels.**

Say the word on each frog. Find a word that rhymes with it from the word bank. Write the rhyming word on the log.

boy	can	day
hop	kiss	tent
town	tree	two

1.  ran

2. you

3. she

4. went

5. top

6. ray

7. down

8. toy

9. miss

Make your own rhyming words!

10. *pat* rhymes with ____at

11. *lot* rhymes with ____ot

12. *dip* rhymes with ____ip

13. *fed* rhymes with ____ed

14. *sub* rhymes with ____ub

❑ **I can name words that rhyme.**

K.RF.2c

Cut out each letter at the bottom of the page. Paste each letter in the correct box to make rhyming words.

☐ I can rhyme single syllable words.
☐ I can put together word parts.
☐ I can take apart word parts.

m   c   n

There are five main vowels: *a, e, i, o,* and *u.*
The short vowel sounds are:
    <u>a</u> as in c<u>a</u>t   <u>e</u> as in b<u>e</u>d   i as in h<u>i</u>p   <u>o</u> as in t<u>o</u>p   <u>u</u> as in t<u>u</u>b

Complete each word with the correct sound. Color each gumball. Use the color key.

Color Key
a = yellow
e = orange
i = red
o = blue
u = green

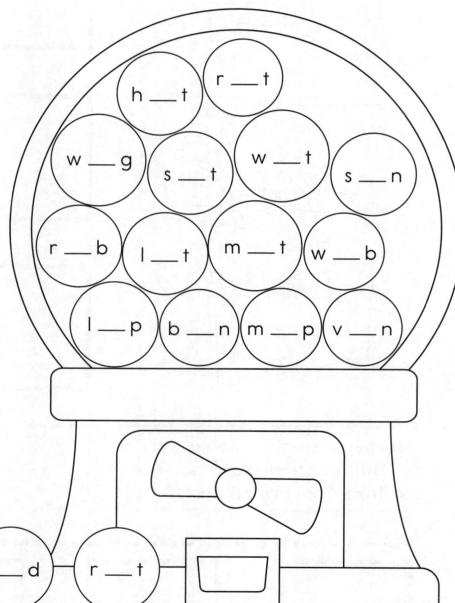

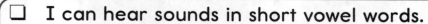

❑ **I can hear sounds in short vowel words.**
❑ **I can recognize words with short vowel sounds.**

Complete each word with the correct short vowel sound.

 1. c ____ p

 2. d ____ t

 3. l ____ g

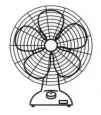 4. f ____ n

 5. m ____ p

 6. l ____ ps

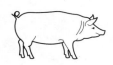 7. p ____ g

 8. h ____ t

 9. n ____ t

 10. tr ____ ck

❑ **I can pronounce sounds of words.**
❑ **I can recognize vowels.**

Words can be "chopped" into sounds.
The word *mud* has three sounds: /m/, /u/, /d/.

Karate chop each word. Draw a line after each sound in the word.

Example: b | u | s |

1. o n

2. u p

3. w i g

4. b a t

5. a n t

6. w i n

7. b e d

8. j e t

9. s l e d

10. p l a n

☐   **I can say each sound in a word.**

Cut out the letters at the bottom of the page. Paste them in the correct boxes to complete the rhyming words.

Change the vowel in each word to make a new word. The vowels are *a, e, i, o,* and *u.*

Old Words	New Words
red	
tin	
mess	

❑ **I can rhyme.**
❑ **I can make new words by changing the vowel.**

✂ - ✂

g   cl   fr

Change the first letter of each word to make a new word. Write the new word.

1. bet _____

2. hip _____

3. fish _____

4. bud _____

5. sit _____

6. top _____

Change the second letter of each word to make a new word. You will need to use the vowels a, e, i, o, and u. Write the new word.

7. bag _____

8. hid _____

9. went _____

10. dig _____

11. sing _____

12. tell _____

Change the last letter of each word to make a new word. Write the new word.

13. tan _____

14. lid _____

15. beg _____

16. fig _____

17. man _____

18. pat _____

☐ **I can change letters in a word to make a new word.**
☐ **I can make new words.**

Say the name of each picture. Circle the letter that makes the beginning sound.

1. m p	2. t r	3. y q
4. f r	5. v x	6. a o
7. v p	8. s z	9. w n

☐ **I can use phonics to decode words.**

Name_____

Say the name of each picture. Circle the letter that makes the ending sound.

1. m   t
2. d   g
3. t   l
4. n   s
5. t   c
6. j   t
7. i   m
8. g   f
9. l   j

☐ I can use phonics to decode words.

Name_____

We can put words in order. A group of words can be put in the order of the alphabet by their first letters. This is called *alphabetical order.*

1. Look at the first letter of each word.

2. Decide which letter comes first in the alphabet.

3. Write this word.

4. Continue until you use all of the words.

<u>c</u>at, <u>b</u>at, <u>f</u>at   b   <u>b</u>at   <u>b</u>at, <u>c</u>at, <u>f</u>at

Write the words on the cones in alphabetical order.

1._____

2._____

3._____

man
can
tan

3._____

4._____

5._____

tree
grass
sky

6._____

7._____

8._____

four
one
nine

❑ **I can notice the sounds in words.**
❑ **I can put words in alphabetical order.**
❑ **I know the sounds of consonants.**

Name_____

Read each word. Write an e after each word. Read the
new word.

1. can____

2. cap____

3. dim____

4. fad____

5. fin____

6. hop____

7. mad____

8. man____

9. mop____

10. not____

11. pal____

12. pan____

13. pin____

14. tap____

❑ **I can notice long and short vowel sounds in words.**
❑ **I know the five major vowels and the sounds.**

Find two partners. Write your name on top of the first column. Write your partners' names on the tops of the other columns. Read your words aloud. Listen to your partners read theirs.

Name:	Name:	Name:
a	boy	from
after	brother	girl
all	car	give
am	children	go
and	come	good
animal	did	have
are	do	here
at	eat	house
be	favorite	how
because	friend	I

❑ **I can read sight words.**

K.RF.3c

Find two partners. Write your name on top of the first column. Write your partners' names on the tops of the other columns. Read your words aloud. Listen to your partners read theirs.

Name:	Name:	Name:
is	of	sister
jump	off	some
kick	out	talk
like	over	that
make	people	the
me	play	thing
my	pretty	under
new	quit	very
nice	said	was
night	school	you

☐ **I can read sight words.**

> Some words have the same ending sounds. We say they *rhyme*. These words are in the same word family.
>
> Examples: king, ring, sing

Draw a line to match each picture to the correct word family.

1.   og

2.   an

3.   at

4.   en

5.   op

6.   et

7.  ap

8.  ug

Write the correct word family for each picture.

9.   l ____ ____

10.   n ____ ____

11.   c ____ ____

12.   b ____ ____

☐ **I can identify different letter sounds.**
☐ **I can understand word families.**
☐ **I can identify words with letter sounds that differ.**

Read each poem four times.

The fat cat
sat on the hat.
The hat went flat.
"Meow, meow!" said the cat.

The white dog barks.
The green bird sings.
The orange cat meows.
The yellow lion roars.

☐ **I can understand what I read.**

Think of a place you want to visit.

1. Draw the place that you want to visit.

2. Write a sentence.

I want to visit_____ because_____

_____.

3. Draw a picture of the fun things you can do in this place.

☐ **I can draw and write about something I like.**
☐ **I can draw and write to show others what I think.**

Read each topic. Draw a picture in each box. Think about how you can show feelings.

a kind child	a nice dog
a proud mom	a shy student

Choose your favorite topic. Write a sentence.

_____

_____

❑ I can draw and write about what I think.
❑ I can draw and write about my opinion.

> A **complete sentence** tells a thought. The words are in the correct order. The sentence makes sense.
>
>   Example: Maria walks to the store.
>
> A **fragment** is not a complete sentence. It does not tell a thought.
>
>   Example: Walks to the store.

Fix each fragment. Make a complete sentence.

1. bake cookies

   _____

2. the garden

   _____

3. is red and white

   _____

4. apples and pears

   _____

5. rides the bus

   _____

❏ **I can write complete sentences with information.**

Look at the pictures. Number the pictures 1, 2, or 3 in the order they would happen.

1.

_____   _____   _____

2.

_____   _____   _____

3.

_____   _____   _____

❑ **I can put events in order.**

Draw a picture of a special time or event when you felt happy.

Why did you feel happy? Write a sentence.

_____

_____

- ❑ **I can draw and write about a time or event.**
- ❑ **I can tell about an event.**
- ❑ **I can tell how I feel.**

Poetry lets us read and write words in special ways. An acrostic poem spells a word. The word is a topic. Each letter starts a word.

Example: F ull moon
U nder
N ight

Write an acrostic poem about a season. Choose summer, winter, autumn, or spring. Spell the word. Use each letter to make a word about the season.

_____ _____

_____ _____

_____ _____

_____ _____

_____ _____

_____ _____

Share your poem with a partner. Ask your partner to help you make your writing better. Fix your poem.

- ☐ **I can write a poem.**
- ☐ **I can get help from classmates.**
- ☐ **I can make my writing better.**

Write an acrostic poem about a family member. Spell his or her name. Use each letter to make a new word about the person.

Draw a picture of the person.

___ _____   ___ _____

___ _____   ___ _____

___ _____   ___ _____

___ _____   ___ _____

___ _____   ___ _____

___ _____   ___ _____

___ _____   ___ _____

___ _____   ___ _____

___ _____   ___ _____

Share your poem with a partner. Ask your partner to help you make your writing better. Fix your poem.

❑ **I can write a poem.**
❑ **I can get help from classmates.**
❑ **I can make my writing better.**

Journal writing is a way to share ideas and feelings.

Read each prompt. Add words and pictures.

I am happy when . . .

I feel tired when . . .

I get excited when . . .

Choose one of your prompts. Add a sentence to it. Type it on a computer.

❑ **I can write about thoughts and feelings.**
❑ **I can publish my writing.**

Everyone has different likes and dislikes. Read the titles of the lists. Write about yourself under each title.

Things I Can Do

1. _____

2. _____

3. _____

Games I Like to Play

1. _____

2. _____

3. _____

Places I Have Been

1. _____

2. _____

3. _____

Choose one of your topics. Write three complete sentences. Use a separate sheet of paper. Have a partner look at your writing. Ask your partner to help you make your writing better. Fix your writing. Type it on a computer.

❑ I can fix my writing with a friend.
❑ I can publish my writing.

Find a partner. Ask your partner the questions. Write your partner's answers.

1. What is your name?

_____

2. What is your favorite color?

_____

3. What do you like to do in school?

_____

4. What do you like to do at home?

_____

5. What do you like to do outside?

_____

Type your sentences on a computer. Print them. Draw a picture of your partner below your story.

☐   I can work with a partner on writing.
☐   I can publish my writing.

Read the story "Cinderella." It is a fairy tale. The prince is looking for a woman. She lost her glass slipper.

Report the facts. Complete the chart. Use pictures, words, and sentences. Use the 5 W's. The 5 W's are *who*, *what*, *where*, *when*, and *why*.

1. What happened?
2. Who was there?
3. When did it happen?
4. Where did it happen?
5. Why did it happen?

☐ **I can research and write.**
☐ **I can use question words.**

Name_____

Explore books by your favorite author. Read the pages of three books. Look at the pictures. Think about why you like each book.

My Favorite Author: _____

Title:

How I feel about this book:

Title:

How I feel about this book:

Title:

How I feel about this book:

☐ **I can research and write.**

Characters are people in a story. Animals can be characters too. Authors make stories with characters.

Choose a character from a book. Draw the character's face. Name the character. Answer the questions. Ask for help if you need it.

_____
Character's Name

1. What does the character look like?

_____

_____

_____

_____

2. What does the character like?

_____

_____

_____

_____

3. What does the character not like?

_____

_____

_____

_____

4. What does the character do for fun?

_____

_____

_____

_____

❏ **I can gather information.**

A **noun** is a word. It can be a person, a place, a thing, or an idea.

Complete the chart with the different kinds of nouns.

Person	Place	Thing	Idea
aunt	home	apple	love

A **verb** is an action word. It shows action.

Complete the chart with verbs.

run	

❑   **I can write nouns and verbs.**

76

A **plural noun** is more than one person, place, thing, or idea. You can make a noun plural by adding an *-s* to the end of a noun.

Example: dog, dog<u>s</u>

Make each noun plural.

1. truck	
2. bear	
3. paper	
4. book	
5. lamp	

Draw one of the plural nouns.

❑ **I can make plural nouns.**

Write a question word from the bank next to each answer.

| who   what   where   when   why   how |

Question Words	Answers
1.	We go at 8:00 in the morning.
2.	I get there by bus.
3.	We will ride to town.
4.	I have to get school clothes.
5.	I go with Aunt Melinda.
6.	We will shop.

❏ **I can use and understand question words.**

A **preposition** is a type of word. It shows how a noun connects to another word in the sentence.

| to | from | for | by | with |

Use the prepositions to complete each sentence.

1. Scott went _____ his friend's yard.

2. Liza can go to school _____ bus.

3. I saw Mom at home _____ Dad.

4. You got a gift _____ your uncle.

5. The card is _____ Kami.

Use a preposition in a sentence.

6. _____

_____

❏ **I can use prepositions.**

Name_____

A **conjunction** is a word that puts words together. It can make a sentence longer.

Example: Amy likes eggs. Amy likes pancakes.

Amy likes eggs <u>and</u> pancakes.

Choose a conjunction from the word bank. Use it to write a sentence about your two favorite snacks. Draw a picture of your sentence.

| and | or | but |

_____

_____

❑ **I can expand sentences.**

The first letter in a sentence is a capital letter. Write each sentence correctly.

1. will Wendy run in the race?

_____

2. sydney rides her bike.

_____

The letter *i* is a capital *I* when it is alone. Write each sentence correctly.

3. nora and i sat on the couch.

_____

4. fay and i see the mountains!

_____

Ending punctuation stops a sentence. There are three types.

A **statement** gives information. It ends with a period.	A **question** asks something. It ends with a question mark.	An **exclamation** shows strong feelings. It ends with an exclamation point.

Read each sentence. Circle the one with the correct punctuation.

5. A. Watch out for the hole.

   B. Watch out for the hole!

6. A. Please pass the butter.

   B. Please pass the butter?

7. A. Where are you going?

   B. Where are you going.

❑ I can can capitalize the first word in a sentence.
❑ I can capitalize the pronoun *I*.
❑ I can name ending punctuation.

Some words are spelled alike and sound alike but have different meanings. We know which meaning makes sense when we read the rest of the sentence.

Examples: I turned on the <u>fan</u>.

The <u>fan</u> cheered.

Read each pair of sentences. Write the word from the word bank that makes sense in both sentences.

| back | bark | roll | saw | star |

1. Matt _____ a lion at the zoo.

   Dad cut the tree with a _____.

2. The _____ on the tree was brown.

   Listen to the big dog _____.

3. Jan was the _____ of the show.

   She drew a _____ on her paper.

4. I ate a _____ at lunch.

   Sam will _____ the ball to her.

5. Ann shut the _____ door.

   Tim swam on his _____.

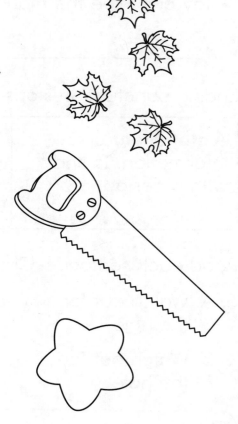

☐ **I can find the meaning of words in sentences.**

Read each pair of sentences. Write the word from the word bank that makes sense in both sentences.

| feet | jam | leaves | light | spring |

1. The days grow warmer, and _____ comes.

   We watched the rabbit _____ onto the log.

2. The wood is three _____ long.

   The hot sand is burning my _____.

3. I tried to _____ my toys into the box.

   She eats grape _____.

4. At 3:00 pm, my teacher _____ school.

   The colorful _____ fall from the trees.

5. The sun's _____ warms my face.

   The empty bag felt _____.

❏ **I can learn new meanings of words.**

> A **prefix** is a part of a word. It is at the beginning of many words. It is a syllable.

Add the correct prefix from the word bank to each word below. Write the meaning.

re-	**sub-**	**un-**
again	under	not

1. _____marine : _____

2. _____tie : _____

3. _____do : _____

> A **suffix** is a part of a word. It is at the end of many words. It can be a syllable.

Add the correct suffix from the word bank to each word below. Write the meaning.

-er	**-ful**	**-less**
a person who	full of	without

4. play_____ : _____

5. hope_____ : _____

6. work_____ : _____

> ☐ **I can use a prefix as a clue to the meaning of a word.**
> ☐ **I can use a suffix as a clue to the meaning of a word.**

Each word has a meaning. Two words can mean almost the same thing. These are called **synonyms**.

Draw a line to match each word with its synonym.

1. toss   tear

2. thin   throw

3. rip   skinny

4. big   small

5. tiny   large

Choose one pair of synonyms. Write a sentence with each word.

6. _____

7. _____

Draw a picture of one of your sentences.

❑ **I can understand similar word meanings.**

K.L.5a

Place an X on the word that does not belong in each row.

1.

basketball   tennis racket   football   baseball

2.

lion   dog   fox   fish

3.

shirt   shoe   crayon   hat

4.

soup   tree   cake   apple

❑   I can sort objects into groups.

> **Adjectives** are describing words. They describe nouns.
>
> Example: The apple is **big**.

Draw a line to match the opposite adjectives.

1. The cake is **big**.

The boy is **sad**.

2. The ball is **high**.

The cake is **little**.

3. The boy is **happy**.

The ball is **low**.

> **Verbs** are action words.

Draw a line to match the opposite verbs.

4. catch	go
5. stop	drop
6. lay	stand

☐ **I can match words to their opposites.**

Read the words in the word bank. Circle each object in the house.

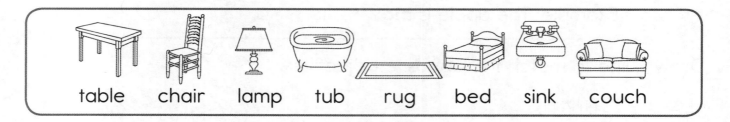

table   chair   lamp   tub   rug   bed   sink   couch

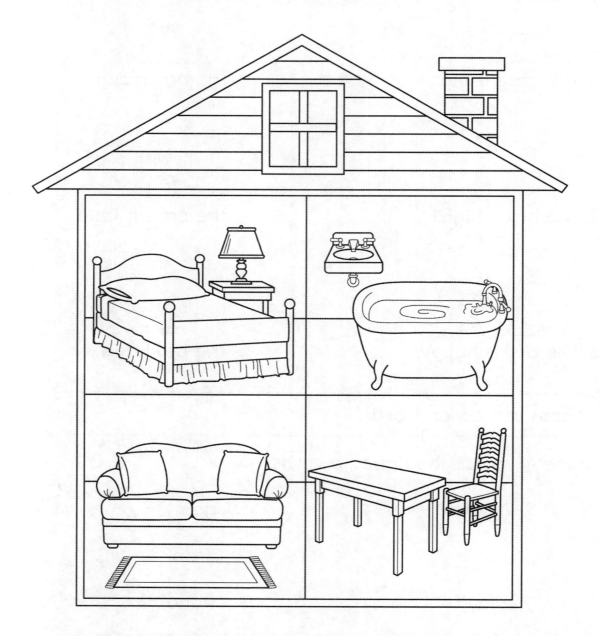

☐   **I can connect words to how they are used in real life.**

Words have shades of meaning. Find a partner. Perform each group of words. Have fun!

1.	walk	march	prance
2.	whisper	talk	shout
3.	look	stare	glance
4.	pat	tap	poke
5.	jump	skip	hop

6. Draw each word to show how they are different.

big	huge	giant

❑ **I can act out words to show I understand what they mean.**

Your teacher will read you a story. Listen to the story. Write the title of the story in the center box. Write words and phrases from the story in the boxes.

	Title of the Story _____ _____	

Find a partner. Talk about what you heard in the story. Use your words and phrases from the boxes.

❑ **I can listen to a story.**
❑ **I can use words and phrases from the story.**

Answer Key

Page 12
1. Mom and Ryan; 2. oranges;
3. the grocery store; 4. after
mom parked the car; 5. happy

Page 13
1. red; 2. balls and sticks;
3. teeth

Page 14
1. He watched the sheep. He
became bored. 2. He told the
villagers there was a wolf. He
was sorry. 3. The villagers did
not believe him.

Page 15
1. picture of characters should
include a boy and villagers;
2. picture of setting should
include hills, grass, and village
at the bottom of hill; 3. Answers
will vary.

Page 16
1. a type of flower; 2. dirt; 3. an
herb

Page 17
Drawings will vary but may
include a porch, cars, birds, a
book, a mailman, a letter, wind,
a sweater, a neighbor, or
the sun.

Page 18
1. Both have characters, a
setting, and events. 2. Poems
can rhyme and may not have
complete sentences.

Page 19
1-3. Answers will vary.

Page 20
1. Both girls like to jump rope,
swim, and ride bikes. 2. Kris likes

to wear shorts, belts, and bows
in her hair. 3. Kim likes to wear
skirts, sandals, and to wear her
hair down.

Page 21
1. Answers will vary. 2. Answers
will vary. 3. They are alike
because they want to run
and win the race. 4. They are
different because the hare was
fast and took a break, and the
turtle was slow and steady.

Page 22
Drawings will vary.

Page 23
Drawings will vary.

Page 24
1. Answers will vary. 2. Answers
will vary but should match the
underlined sentence.
3. Observe sharing with a
friend.

Page 25
1. the school playground;
2. slide, monkey bars, ladders,
sandbox; 3. Answers will vary.

Page 26
1. A; 2. C; 3. D; 4. B

Page 27
Answers will vary but may
include Planting Seeds, Playing
with a Friend, Buying a Puppy,
or Playing in the Rain.

Page 28
1. a cold-blooded animal with
scales; 2. square, hard pieces
that cover the snake's body.
3. a warm, wet place where
snakes live

Page 29
Answers will vary.

Page 30
Answers will vary.

Page 31
1. bear; 2. fish; 3. rabbit;
4. octopus

Page 32
1. Bats keep bugs away from us.
2. Bats are also very interesting.

Page 33
1. Drawings will vary.
2. Drawings will vary.
3. Answers will vary but should
focus on safety. 4. Answers will
vary but should include the
difference between wearing a
helmet versus gloves.

Page 34
Answers will vary.

Page 35
1. My sister is over there.
2. Have you seen my
backpack? 3. We go to
the park.

Page 36
Answers will vary.

Page 37
Answers will vary.

Page 38
Answers will vary.

Page 39
1. I see three apples. 2. It is a
triangle. 3. The paint is red.

Answer Key

Page 40
Answers and drawings will vary.

Page 41
Answers and drawings will vary.

Page 42
Answers will vary.

Page 43
Answers will vary.

Page 44
1. 2, 2; 2. 1, 1; 3. 1, 1; 4. 2, 2; 5. 3, 3; 6. 2, 2; 7. 2, 2; 8. 3, 3; 9. 1, 1; 10. 1, 1; 1 syllable: three, red, nine, truck; 2 syllables: brother, sister, pretty, under; 3 syllables: elephant, favorite

Page 45
can, fan; lamb, jam; tag, flag; rake, cake; 1. 2; 2. 2; 3. 1; 4. 1; 5. 1; 6. 2

Page 46
1. red: hat, sat, bat, that; 2. yellow: top, mop, pop; 3. green: led, red, sled; 4. blue: jug, rug, hug; 5. Colors will vary.

Page 47
1. cake, rake; 2. bone, cone; 3. pie, tie; 4. tire, fire; 5. gate, skate

Page 48
1. can; 2. two; 3. tree; 4. tent; 5. hop; 6. day; 7. town; 8. boy; 9. kiss; 10. Answers will vary but may include mat. 11. Answers will vary but may include cot. 12. Answers will vary but may include hip. 13. Answers will vary but may include red.

14. Answers will vary but may include tub.

Page 49
cap; nap; map

Page 50
Words will vary but may include hat, hit, or hut; rat, rot, or rut; wag or wig; sat, set, or sit; wit or wet; sin, son, or sun; rib, rob, or rub; let, lit, or lot; mat or met; web; lap, lip, or lop; ban, bin, or bun; map or mop; van; red or rid; rat, rot, or rut.

Page 51
1. cup; 2. dot; 3. leg; 4. fan; 5. mop; 6. lips; 7. pig; 8. net; 9. hat; 10. truck

Page 52
1. o | n; 2. u | p; 3. w | i | g; 4. b | a | t; 5. a | n | t; 6. w | i | n; 7. b | e | d; 8. j | e | t; 9. s | l | e | d; 10. p | l | a | n

Page 53
crown; gown; frown; Answers will vary but may include rid or rod; tan, ten, or ton; and mass, miss, moss, or muss.

Page 54
1. Answers will vary but may include get, jet, let, met, net, pet, set, vet, wet, yet. 2. Answers will vary but may include dip, lip, nip, rip, sip, tip, zip. 3. Answers will vary but may include dish, wish. 4. Answers will vary but may include dud, mud. 5. Answers will vary but may include bit, fit, hit, kit, lit, nit, pit, wit. 6. Answers will vary but may include bop, cop, hop, lop, mop, pop, sop. 7. Answers

will vary but may include beg, big, bog, bug. 8. had; 9. want; 10. Answers will vary but may include dog, dug. 11. Answers will vary but may include sang, song, sung. 12. Answers will vary but may include tall, till, toll. 12. Answers will vary but may include tab, tag, tan, tap, tar. 13. Answers will vary but may include lie, lip, lit. 14. Answers will vary but may include bed, Ben, bet. 15. Answers will vary but may include fib, fin, fit, fix. 16. Answers will vary but may include mad, map, mat, Max, may. 17. Answers will vary but may include pad, pal, pan, paw, pay.

Page 55
1. M; 2. T; 3. Q; 4. R; 5. V; 6. O; 7. P; 8. S; 9. N

Page 56
1. T; 2. G; 3. L; 4. N; 5. T; 6. T; 7. M; 8. G; 9. L

Page 57
1. can; 2. man; 3. tan; 4. grass; 5. sky; 6. tree; 7. four; 8. nine; 9. one

Page 58
1. cane; 2. cape; 3. dime; 4. fade; 5. fine; 6. hope; 7. made; 8. mane; 9. mope; 10. note; 11. pale; 12. pane; 13. pine; 14. tape

Page 61
1. og; 2. op; 3. at; 4. ap; 5. an; 6. en; 7. ug; 8. et; 9. og; 10. et; 11. an; 12. ee

Page 63
1–3. Answers will vary.

92

Answer Key

Page 64
Answers will vary.

Page 65
1–5. Answers will vary, but sentences must include a subject and verb to be complete.

Page 66
1. 2, 3, 1; 2. 2, 1, 3; 3. 3, 2, 1

Page 67
Answers will vary.

Page 68
Answers will vary.

Page 69
Answers will vary.

Page 70
Answers will vary.

Page 71
Answers will vary.

Page 72
Answers will vary.

Page 73
1. Answers will vary but may include that Cinderella lost her slipper. 2. Answers will vary but may include that people were at the ball with the prince. 3. It happened at night. 4. It happened at the ball. 5. Answers will vary.

Page 74
Answers will vary.

Page 75
Answers will vary.

Page 76
Answers will vary.

Page 77
1. trucks; 2. bears; 3. papers; 4. books; 5. lamps; Answers will vary.

Page 78
1. when; 2. how; 3. where; 4. why; 5. who; 6. what

Page 79
1. to; 2. by; 3. with; 4. for or from; 5. for or from; 6. Answers will vary.

Page 80
Answers will vary.

Page 81
1. Will Wendy run in the race?
2. Sydney rides her bike.
3. Nora and I sat on the couch.
4. Fay and I see the mountains!
5. B; 6. A; 7. A

Page 82
1. saw; 2. bark; 3. star; 4. roll; 5. back

Page 83
1. spring; 2. feet; 3. jam; 4. leaves; 5. light

Page 84
1. sub-, underwater vehicle; 2. un-, to take ties apart or re-, to tie again; 3. re-, do again, or un-, to take apart; 4. –ful, in a playing mood or full of play, or -er, one who plays; 5. –less, without hope, or -ful, full of hope; 6. –er, one who works

Page 85
1. throw; 2. skinny; 3. tear; 4. large; 5. small; 6. Answers will vary. 7. Answers will vary.

Page 86
1. tennis racket; 2. fish; 3. crayon; 4. tree

Page 87
1. The cake is little. 2. The ball is low. 3. The boy is sad. 4. drop; 5. go; 6. stand

Page 88
All words should be circled

Page 89
1–6. Answers will vary.

Page 90
Answers will vary.

Notes

Notes

Notes